Maurice an

Volcanologists

By Vanessa Marchetti

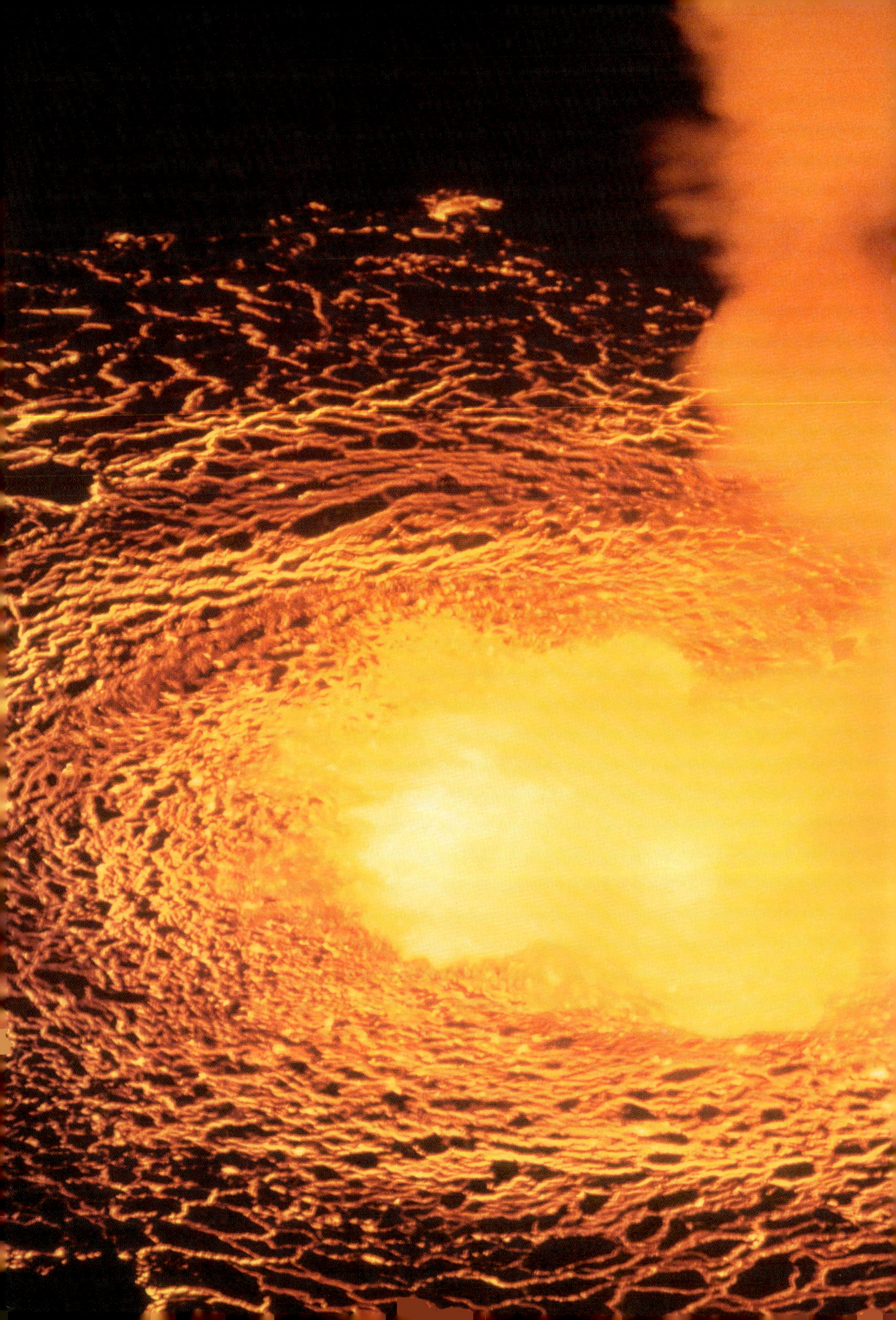

Contents

Hot Work

Imagine gazing down a hole that reaches deep inside the earth. With every breath you take, you're nearly overcome by a stink worse than the smell of rotten eggs.

Imagine crawling past a river of **lava.** As the lava rushes by, it hisses and bubbles and you fear that the ground beneath you might crumble at any minute.

These images may seem like scenes from an exciting movie. But for **volcanologists** Maurice and Katia Krafft, moments like these were all in a day's work.

Maurice and Katia Krafft

Maurice Krafft at work on an active volcano (above); volcanic rock (right)

Volcanologists are scientists that study the many different aspects of volcanoes. Some volcanologists might never visit a volcano. Instead, they work in a **laboratory** and study volcanic rocks. By looking at these rocks, volcanologists can learn how a volcano acted while it erupted. Other volcanologists may study only **dormant,** or inactive, volcanoes. Dormant volcanoes can help scientists understand past eruptions and the earth's history.

The study of **active volcanoes** is the most direct—and dangerous—way to learn about volcanoes. By watching volcanoes as they erupt, volcanologists can learn why volcanoes erupt and how to predict future eruptions. Volcanologists Maurice and Katia Krafft loved the thrill and adventure of standing beside an erupting volcano. They dedicated their lives to the study of active volcanoes around the world.

Volcanoes 101

A volcano is an opening in the earth where **magma**, or liquid rock, can come to the surface from deep in the earth and form new rock. The hot magma causes gases to form that can make the volcano erupt. Sometimes the magma pours out onto the earth as lava. Sometimes the eruption sends ash into the air. A volcano can erupt many times. Volcanoes come in different shapes:

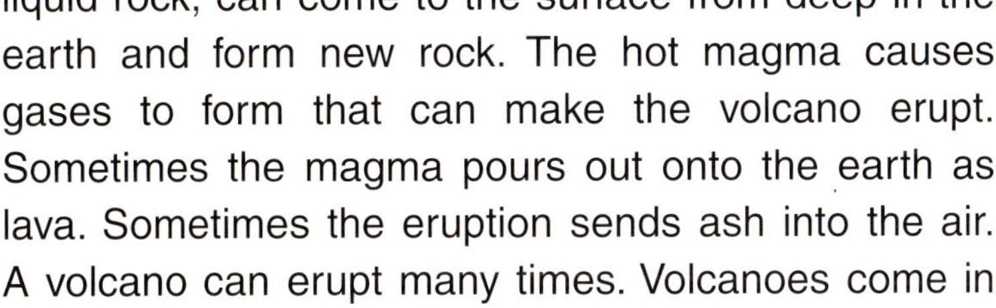

Composite **Cinder** **Shield**

Young Scientists

The volcano Stromboli is near the island of Sicily in Italy.

At an early age, both Maurice and Katia Krafft knew that they wanted to study volcanoes. In 1954, when Maurice was seven years old, his father took him to Italy to see the volcano Stromboli erupt. Maurice was amazed by the fiery mountain and wanted to learn more.

After his trip to Stromboli, Maurice returned home to France. The only volcanoes in France are very old and do not erupt anymore. So Maurice made models of volcanoes. He studied rocks from ancient volcanoes near his home. By the time he was fifteen, Maurice was a member of the French Geological Society and on his way to becoming a scientist.

Make Your Own Volcanic Eruption

First, make sure you have an adult helping you before starting this experiment. Then follow these steps below:

1. Find an empty plastic bottle, like an old soda bottle.
2. Put the plastic bottle in a sink or tub or in your backyard. (If you want to make it look like a volcano, you could dig a hole in the ground that would hold half of the bottle, and then build a "mountain" of dirt around the mouth of the bottle.)
3. Fill a third of the bottle with white vinegar. Mix in a few drops of red food coloring so it looks like lava.
4. In a liquid measuring cup, mix a half cup of water with a tablespoon of baking soda.
5. Pour the mixture into the plastic bottle and quickly stand back.
6. Watch your volcano erupt!

Katia was fascinated by volcanoes before she ever saw an eruption. As a child in France, she read books about volcanoes and studied the exciting pictures. When she was fourteen years old, she saw her first volcanic eruption, also at Stromboli in Italy. Katia later went to college to learn more about **geology** and volcanoes.

In college she met Maurice. After they graduated, they were married, and together they began to travel the world to study volcanoes.

Volcano Hopping

Today there are more than five hundred active volcanoes in the world. Maurice and Katia visited more than three hundred of these during their lifetimes.

The Kraffts knew people throughout the world who would call them within five minutes of a volcanic eruption. Maurice and Katia always had their equipment packed and ready to go. Volcanic eruptions are difficult to predict and eruptions can begin and end quickly. The Kraffts never wanted to miss any of the action.

Once, they got a call to see an eruption in Iceland. After the eruption, as they got ready to go home, they got a call to go to Hawaii. And from Hawaii, they went to Indonesia to watch another volcano there. In one year they circled the world eight times!

Volcanoes Around the World

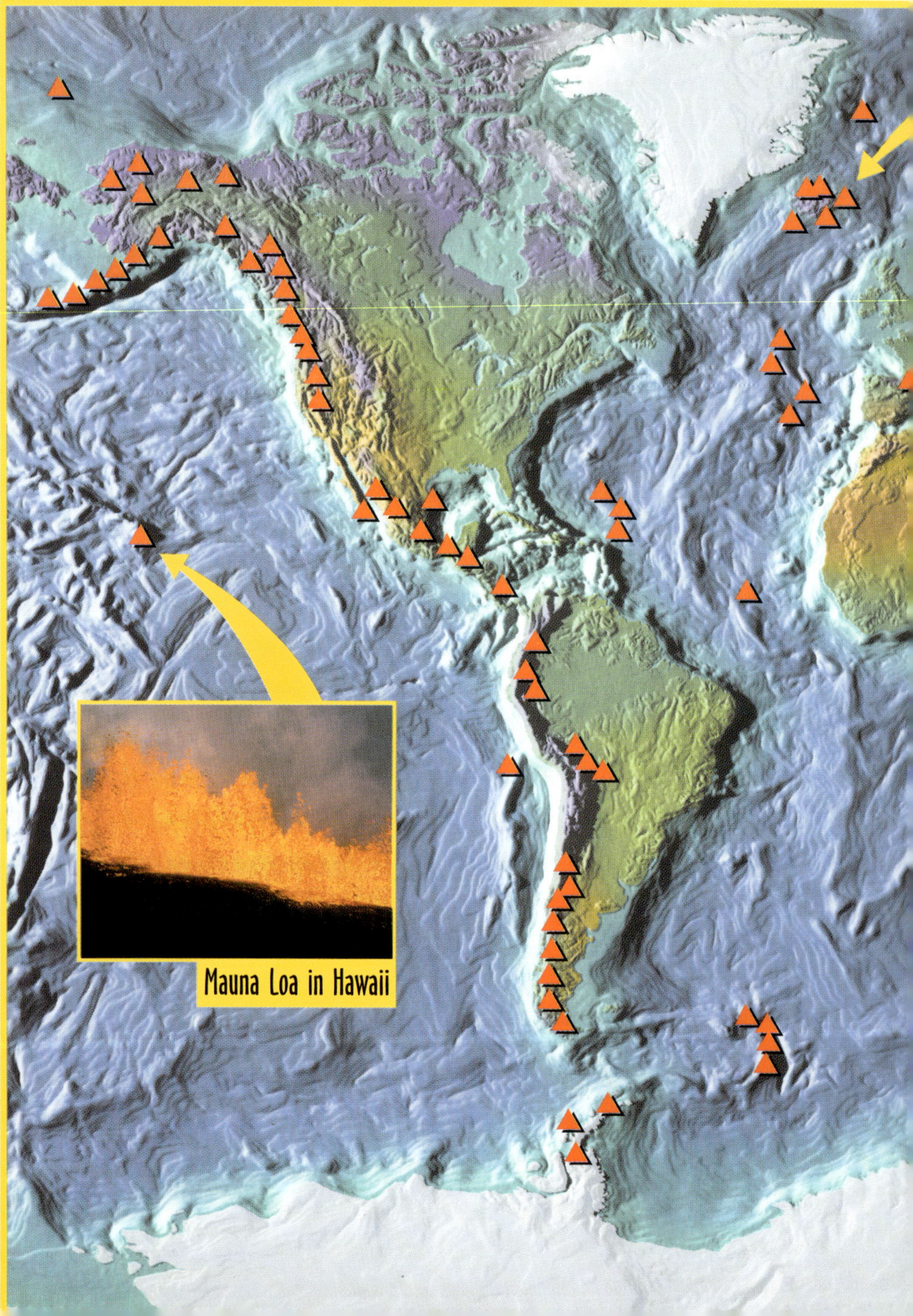

Mauna Loa in Hawaii

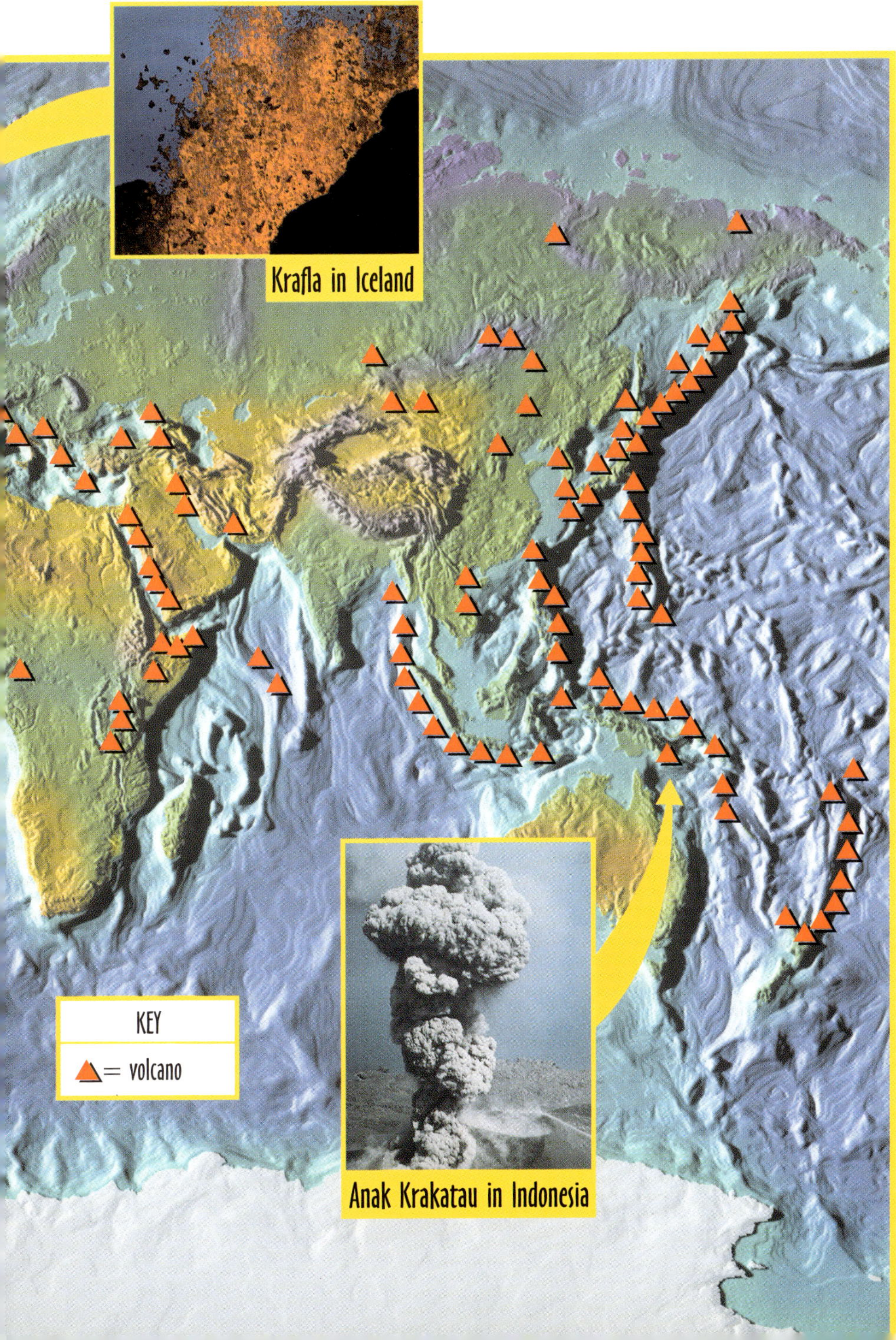

Krafla in Iceland

Anak Krakatau in Indonesia

To study an active volcano, the Kraffts had to get very close to the eruption. They would collect samples of rock and gases and take the lava's temperature with a tool called a **thermocouple.**

Tricks of the Trade

Volcanologists study volcanoes in many ways. They use tools to measure changes in a volcano.

They collect samples of lava and rocks and study them later in a laboratory.

They talk to people who live in the area and who saw changes in the volcano or saw an eruption.

They watch a volcano erupt and take many notes.

They also might study rocks from past eruptions. These rocks can show how a volcano acted when it erupted.

Caution: Falling rocks!

Being close to an eruption is very dangerous. The lava can be hotter than 2,000 degrees Fahrenheit, and the gases that come from an eruption can be deadly. Sometimes these gases made holes in the Kraffts' pants. As they worked, Maurice and Katia would patch the holes with thick white tape. They would wear **gas masks** to keep from breathing in the gases and volcanic ash. And they also wore helmets to protect their heads from falling rocks.

As time passed, **asbestos suits** were made to keep volcanologists like Maurice and Katia safer on volcanoes. The suits have a metal coating and reflect the lava's heat. In these suits Maurice and Katia looked like astronauts on Earth!

After they finished their research on a volcano, the Kraffts would carefully study their notes and samples. Then they might write an article or give a speech to other scientists about the eruptions.

Tools of the Trade

When a volcano is active, it gives off gases; there are also **earthquakes,** and the land around the volcano can swell. Volcanologists use different tools to help them study these changes; these tools can also warn scientists when and where an eruption might occur.

A **correlation spectrometer** is an instrument that measures changes in gases. Changes in the types and amount of gases that a volcano gives off can warn scientists about coming eruptions.

A **seismometer** measures how strong an earthquake is and can help identify where an earthquake started. It can help scientists find where there is a lot of activity under the earth's surface and where a volcanic eruption might occur.

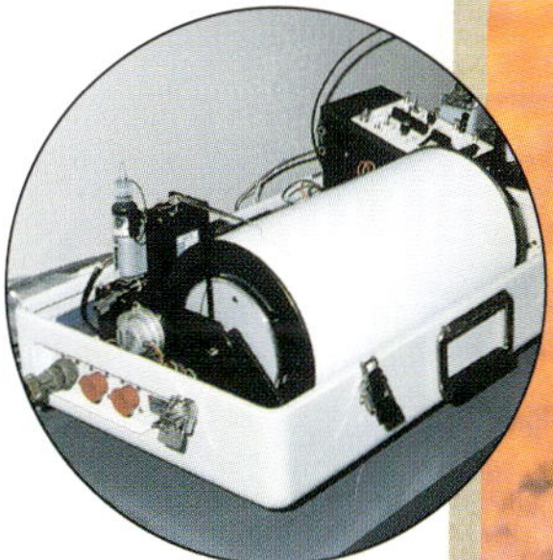

When a volcano is about to erupt, the ground may swell from the pressure of the magma beneath it. A **tiltmeter** is used to determine how much the ground has swelled and where a volcano may erupt.

Always an Adventure

Maurice and Katia had many adventures while studying volcanoes. They traveled to the Great Rift in Africa to study a bubbling pool of lava. There, for the first time in their lives, they hiked deep into a volcano's **crater.** They set up camp in the crater, where they worked for fifteen days. Katia said it was like being inside "the bowels of the earth."

Mt. Nyirangongo in Zaire

One of their wildest adventures was on a volcanic lake in Indonesia known as "The Green Crater." This lake, made of acid, was formed after a volcano erupted. Acid is a liquid that can eat away at many things, including skin! If Maurice and Katia had fallen in the acid lake, their bodies would have dissolved within an hour. They floated out on the lake in an acid-proof rubber boat. Then they carefully took samples of the acid with a bottle attached to the end of a metal cable. When the acid ate through the metal cable, they had to stop taking samples.

An Amazing Show

Even more than taking samples and making notes, Maurice and Katia loved the show of a volcanic eruption. Sometimes they would forget their research as they watched the amazing eruption unfold. Before long, they wanted to share the power and beauty of these eruptions with people around the world.

So the Kraffts began filming and photographing eruptions to capture their beauty. They would return home from their various trips with hours of film and hundreds of photos.

Maurice was in charge of the filmmaking. Katia was the photographer. She would often take many pictures of an eruption from different angles to record all of its details. But she liked taking beautiful pictures of the volcanoes even more.

Katia's photos have been published in such magazines as *National Geographic* and in many books about volcanoes.

Students at the Center for the Study of Active Volcanoes. The Center is part of the University of Hawaii.

Maurice and Katia also made several movies including one called *Understanding Volcanic Hazards.* More than five hundred million people live near volcanoes. The Kraffts hoped that the film would teach these people about the risks of living near a volcano and how they might stay safe during an eruption. The Kraffts believed that people would understand the dangers if they could see it for themselves in a film.

In 1991, not long after making this movie, the Kraffts went to Japan to see an eruption. Volcanoes can be unpredictable, even to volcanologists. Tragically, the Kraffts were caught in a hot ash flow and were killed.

In memory of the Kraffts, the Maurice and Katia Krafft Memorial Fund was formed. It gives travel money to students from other countries so that they can study at the Center for the Study of Active Volcanoes in Hawaii. There, volcanologists teach about the risks of volcanoes and how to monitor eruptions. Like the Kraffts, the students and scientists at the Center are working to help keep people safe during volcanic eruptions.

The Kraffts are remembered as two of the leading volcanologists in the world. Their amazing films, their many photographs, and their valuable research have saved lives and shown the beauty of volcanoes to the world.

Glossary

active volcano: A volcano that is erupting or showing signs of possible eruption.

asbestos suit: Clothing worn to protect a volcanologist.

correlation spectrometer: An instrument used to measure volcanic gases.

crater: A bowl-shaped pit around the mouth of a volcano.

dormant: An inactive or "sleeping" volcano.

earthquake: A movement in the earth.

gas mask: A mask worn over the nose and mouth that prevents a person from breathing toxic air.

geology: The study of rocks and rock history.

laboratory: A place where scientists conduct tests.

lava: Hot liquid rock (magma) that has broken through the earth's surface.

magma: Hot liquid rock beneath the earth's surface.

seismometer: An instrument used to measure earthquakes.

thermocouple: An instrument used to measure the temperature of lava.

tiltmeter: An instrument used to measure the tilting and swelling of land.

volcanologists: Scientists that specialize in the study of volcanoes.